UNMASKING THE SKUNK APE:

A Deep Dive into America's Elusive Creature

Synopsis:

For decades, reports of an elusive and mysterious creature known as the Skunk Ape have surfaced in the swamps and forests of America. With its foul smell and large, hairy frame, the Skunk Ape has become a legend in its own right, but its existence remains shrouded in mystery.
In this book, we'll delve into the history, sightings, and legends surrounding the Skunk Ape, exploring the possible origins of this enigmatic creature and the scientific evidence that has been collected over the years.

From the legends of Native American tribes to modern-day eyewitness accounts, we'll take a journey through the world of the Skunk Ape, examining the evidence and separating fact from fiction.

We'll also investigate the cultural impact of the Skunk Ape, from its depiction in pop culture to its potential impact on tourism in the areas where it is said to roam.

Finally, we'll explore the possible explanations for the Skunk Ape's existence, from the idea that it is a yet-undiscovered species to the possibility that it is a creature that has been brought to life through the power of folklore.

With in-depth analysis, Unmasking the Skunk Ape offers a fascinating look at one of America's most enduring mysteries, leaving readers to decide for themselves whether the Skunk Ape is a true creature of the wild or simply a product of our imagination.

CHAPTER 1:
INTRODUCTION

What is the Skunk Ape?

The Skunk Ape is a mysterious cryptid that is said to inhabit the swamps and forests of Florida, and has been the subject of much speculation and folklore for decades. This creature is often described as a large, hairy, bipedal creature with a distinct odor, similar to that of a skunk, hence the name "Skunk Ape". Sightings and encounters with the Skunk Ape have been reported for centuries, with many people claiming to have seen the creature or found evidence of its presence, such as footprints, hair samples, and unusual vocalizations.

Despite the numerous sightings and evidence, there is still a great deal of skepticism about the existence of the Skunk Ape, with many experts in the fields of science and zoology dismissing it as a myth or hoax. However, there are also many researchers and enthusiasts who believe that the Skunk Ape could be a real, undiscovered species of primate, and have dedicated their lives to studying and investigating the creature.

In this book, we will explore the fascinating world of the Skunk Ape, delving into its origins, folklore, scientific investigations, and cultural impact. Through a combination of eyewitness testimonies, scientific research, and analysis of popular culture, we will attempt to unravel the mystery of this enigmatic cryptid and discover what, if anything, lies behind the legend of the Skunk Ape.

HISTORICAL SIGHTINGS AND ENCOUNTERS

The Skunk Ape is more than just a cryptid – it's a legend. For centuries, stories of a giant, hairy creature have circulated among Native American tribes and settlers in the swamps and forests of the southeastern United States. But it wasn't until the 1960s that the Skunk Ape gained national attention, thanks to a series of sightings and reports.

In this chapter, we'll explore the origins of the Skunk Ape legend and the various cultural and historical factors that may have contributed to its creation.

We'll examine the beliefs of Native American tribes, such as the Seminole and Miccosukee, who have long told stories of a creature known as the "swamp ape" or "stink ape." We'll also explore the influence of African folklore and the concept of "wild men" in European legends.

Additionally, we'll look at the impact of early explorers and settlers on the creation of the Skunk Ape legend. The fear of the unknown and the dangers of the wild likely played a role in the development of tales of a large, dangerous creature lurking in the wilderness.

Finally, we'll discuss how the Skunk Ape has been depicted in popular culture, from movies and TV shows to books and music. The creature's popularity as a subject of horror and intrigue has only served to fuel its legend and keep it alive in the public imagination.

By examining the historical and cultural context of the Skunk Ape legend, we can begin to understand how it has become such an enduring part of American folklore. However, the question remains – is there any truth to the stories of the Skunk Ape? In the following chapters, we'll delve deeper into the evidence and try to separate fact from fiction.

SUPERNATURAL ABILITIES

Reports of the Skunk Ape often include descriptions of supernatural abilities, which have been attributed to the creature by eyewitnesses and storytellers alike. These abilities range from the seemingly mundane to the outright bizarre and have added to the intrigue and mystique surrounding the creature.

One of the most common supernatural abilities attributed to the Skunk Ape is its ability to elude capture. Despite numerous sightings and searches conducted by experienced trackers, hunters, and scientists, the Skunk Ape has never been successfully captured or studied in a controlled environment. Many eyewitnesses report that the creature seems to have an uncanny ability to vanish into the surrounding wilderness, leaving no trace behind.

Other reports suggest that the Skunk Ape may possess some degree of telepathy or mind control. Some eyewitnesses describe feeling as if their minds were being manipulated by the creature, or experiencing strange and vivid hallucinations in its presence. While these reports are difficult to verify, they have contributed to the belief among some researchers that the Skunk Ape may be more than just a simple animal.

In some stories, the Skunk Ape is also said to have supernatural strength and speed. It is reported to be able to run at incredible speeds, easily outrunning even the swiftest of humans. Additionally, some eyewitnesses have reported seeing the creature lift enormous weights or perform other feats of strength that seem to defy explanation.

Finally, some reports suggest that the Skunk Ape may have the ability to disappear or teleport at will. In these stories, witnesses describe seeing the creature vanish into thin air or simply blink out of existence, leaving no trace behind.

While many of these supernatural abilities attributed to the Skunk Ape are difficult to verify, they have contributed to the creature's reputation as a mysterious and powerful force in the wilderness of the southeastern United States. As we delve deeper into the evidence in the following chapters, we'll explore whether these stories are grounded in reality or simply the product of an overactive imagination.

DIFFERENCES BETWEEN THE SKUNK APE AND BIGFOOT

While both the Skunk Ape and Bigfoot are large, hairy, bipedal creatures that are often grouped together as part of the same cryptid family, there are some important differences between the two.

One of the most notable differences is their geographic range. While Bigfoot is typically associated with the Pacific Northwest region of the United States and Canada, the Skunk Ape is primarily reported in the southeastern United States, particularly in Florida. This geographic difference has led some researchers to suggest that the two creatures may actually be separate and distinct species.

Another key difference is their appearance. While

both creatures are typically described as being large, muscular, and covered in hair, the Skunk Ape is often said to have a distinct, foul odor, as its name suggests. This odor has been likened to the smell of rotten eggs or skunk spray and is not commonly associated with reports of Bigfoot sightings.

In addition to their physical differences, the Skunk Ape and Bigfoot also have different cultural and historical contexts. The Skunk Ape has long been a part of the folklore and legends of the southeastern United States, with stories dating back centuries among the Native American tribes of the region. Bigfoot, on the other hand, is a relatively recent addition to the world of cryptozoology, with the first widely reported sightings occurring in the mid-20th century.

Despite these differences, the Skunk Ape and Bigfoot share many similarities and may represent different regional variations of the same basic creature. As we explore the evidence and reports of these cryptids in the following chapters, we'll examine the similarities and differences between them and try to uncover the truth behind these elusive and mysterious creatures.

CHAPTER 2: FOLKLORE AND LEGENDS

The Skunk Ape is deeply rooted in the folklore and history of the southeastern United States, particularly in Florida. The legend of the Skunk Ape has been passed down through generations of Native American tribes, and there are numerous accounts of sightings and encounters dating back centuries.

The Seminole tribe of Florida is particularly associated with the Skunk Ape legend. According to Seminole tradition, the Skunk Ape is a powerful, supernatural creature that lives in the swamps and forests of the region. It is said to be a guardian of the land and a messenger of the gods, with the ability to bestow blessings or curses upon those who encounter it.

One of the earliest recorded sightings of the Skunk Ape occurred in the late 19th century, when a man named Oliver Payne reported seeing a large, hairy creature near Lake Okeechobee. Payne described the creature as being at least 7 feet tall and covered in dark hair, with a strong, musky odor.

Over the years, there have been numerous other reports of Skunk Ape sightings, with many eyewitnesses describing encounters with a creature that matches the same general description. Some reports suggest that the Skunk Ape is a more humanoid creature, while others describe it as being more apelike in appearance.

Despite the many reports of Skunk Ape sightings, there is little concrete evidence to support the existence of the creature. Some researchers believe that the Skunk Ape may be a misidentified known animal, such as a bear or an ape that has escaped from captivity. Others suggest that it may be a completely new species that has yet to be discovered and properly classified by science.

Regardless of the truth behind the Skunk Ape legend, it remains a fascinating and enduring part of American folklore. As we continue to explore the evidence and stories surrounding this mysterious creature in the following chapters, we'll delve deeper into its history and try to uncover the truth behind the legend.

SKUNK APE IN FLORIDA FOLKLORE

The Skunk Ape is deeply rooted in the folklore and legends of the southeastern United States, particularly in Florida. It is said to be a large, hairy, bipedal creature that is known for its distinctive, foul odor, which is said to be similar to the smell of skunk spray or rotten eggs.

The Skunk Ape is deeply ingrained in Florida folklore and has been a part of local legends for centuries. Many Native American tribes, including the Seminole and the Miccosukee, have their own versions of the Skunk Ape legend.

In Seminole folklore, the Skunk Ape is said to be a powerful and sacred creature that has the ability to control the natural elements and bestow blessings or curses upon humans. According to legend, the Skunk Ape appears in times of great change or conflict, as a warning or a message to those who are living out of harmony with nature. It is said that those who are visited by the Skunk Ape are forever changed by the experience and often become spiritual leaders or healers.

The Miccosukee tribe has a slightly different version of the Skunk Ape legend. According to Miccosukee folklore, the Skunk Ape is a shape-shifting creature that can appear in different forms to different people. It is said to be a powerful spirit guide that can help humans navigate the spiritual world and connect with the natural world around them.

In both Seminole and Miccosukee folklore, the Skunk Ape is associated with the swamps and forests of Florida. It is said to be a solitary creature that lives in the most remote and inaccessible parts of the wilderness, and is rarely seen by humans.

Over the years, there have been many reported sightings of the Skunk Ape in Florida, with eyewitnesses describing encounters with a large, hairy creature that matches the general description of the Skunk Ape in folklore. Some researchers believe that these sightings may be the result of misidentified known animals, such as bears or large apes that have escaped from captivity. Others, however, argue that the Skunk Ape may be a completely new species that has yet to be discovered and properly classified by science.

Despite the lack of concrete evidence to support

the existence of the Skunk Ape, its place in Florida folklore remains a fascinating and enduring part of local culture. As we continue to explore the legends and stories surrounding this mysterious creature in the following chapters, we'll delve deeper into its history and try to uncover the truth behind the legend.

The Skunk Ape is not only a part of Native American folklore in Florida, but it has also become a popular topic of discussion and speculation among modern-day cryptozoologists and enthusiasts of the paranormal.

While Florida is perhaps the most well-known location for Skunk Ape sightings, there have been reports of similar creatures in other parts of the United States as well. In some cases, these creatures are referred to as Bigfoot or Sasquatch, but the descriptions of their appearance and behavior often resemble those of the Skunk Ape.

Some reported sightings of the Skunk Ape outside of Florida include those in Louisiana, Georgia, and North Carolina. These sightings often occur in remote and heavily forested areas, where the creature can remain hidden and elusive.

SIMILAR CREATURES IN OTHER CULTURES

The Skunk Ape legend is deeply rooted in the folklore of the southeastern United States, and its origins are difficult to trace. However, there are several common themes that run through many of the stories and legends surrounding this elusive creature.

One of the most striking aspects of the Skunk Ape legend is its odor. According to many eyewitness accounts, the Skunk Ape emits a foul odor, often described as smelling like a mixture of rotten eggs and skunk spray. This detail is consistent across many different reports, and some researchers believe that the odor may actually serve as a way for the creature to communicate or mark its territory.

Another common feature of Skunk Ape stories is its size and appearance. Many reports describe the creature as standing between 6 and 8 feet tall, with broad shoulders and a muscular build. It is typically covered in dark, shaggy fur, and has a distinctive, apelike appearance.

Interestingly, many of the early reports of the Skunk Ape describe it as being more human-like in appearance, with some witnesses even suggesting that it may be a type of undiscovered hominid. However, as the legend has evolved over time, the creature has become more apelike in appearance, which may be due in part to the influence of pop culture representations of Bigfoot and other similar creatures.

Despite the many similarities between Skunk Ape stories, there are also a wide variety of regional and cultural variations. For example, some reports describe the creature as having glowing eyes or supernatural abilities, while others suggest that it is a more mundane creature, simply trying to survive in the harsh wilderness of the southeastern United States.

Regardless of the specific details, the Skunk Ape legend remains a fascinating and enduring part of American folklore. In the following chapters, we'll explore the evidence and try to uncover the truth behind this elusive and mysterious creature.

FOLK EXPLANATIONS FOR THE SKUNK APE

According to the legends and folklore surrounding the Skunk Ape, it is a powerful and supernatural creature that has been associated with a variety of different spiritual beliefs and traditions. For example, the Seminole tribe of Florida believes that the Skunk Ape is a guardian of the land and a messenger of the gods, with the ability to bestow blessings or curses upon those who encounter it.

Other traditions describe the Skunk Ape as a shape-shifter, capable of assuming different forms and appearing to different people in different ways. Some legends also suggest that the Skunk Ape has the ability to control the weather, to predict the future, or to communicate telepathically with humans.

In addition to its supernatural abilities, the Skunk Ape is also associated with a variety of different cultural practices and beliefs. For example, some Native American tribes believe that the Skunk Ape is a spirit guide that can help humans navigate the spiritual world and connect with the natural world around them. Others see the creature as a powerful symbol of the struggle between humanity and the natural world, and as a reminder of the importance of respecting and preserving the environment.

CHAPTER 3: SKUNK APE SIGHTINGS AND ENCOUNTERS

One of the most compelling aspects of the Skunk Ape legend is the number of reported sightings and encounters with the creature over the years. While many of these sightings are likely hoaxes or misidentifications of known animals, some are more difficult to explain and have captured the attention of researchers and enthusiasts alike.

In this chapter, we will explore some of the most famous Skunk Ape sightings and encounters, including eyewitness accounts and physical evidence. We will also examine some of the challenges and limitations of studying these reports, including the reliability of eyewitness testimony and the difficulty of obtaining physical evidence.

Some of the famous sightings and encounters that will be discussed in this chapter include:

The Myakka Skunk Ape Photograph: In 2000, a photograph taken in the Myakka River State Park in Florida appeared to show a large, bipedal, ape-like creature standing in a swampy area. The photograph, which quickly became known as the Myakka Skunk Ape Photograph, has been the subject of much debate and analysis over the years, with some experts suggesting that it may be a hoax or a misidentification of a known animal.

The Green Swamp Encounter: In 2001, a group of hunters in the Green Swamp area of Florida reported a close encounter with a large, hairy, bipedal creature. The hunters claimed that the creature emitted a strong, unpleasant odor and exhibited behavior that was unlike any known animal. While no physical evidence was obtained, the encounter has been cited as one of the most convincing Skunk Ape sightings in recent years.

The Everglades Expedition: In 2013, a team of researchers led by Dave Shealy conducted a month-long expedition in the Florida Everglades in search of the Skunk Ape. The team reported several sightings of large, bipedal creatures that exhibited behavior consistent with the Skunk Ape legend, including tree knocking and vocalizations. While no physical evidence was obtained, the expedition has been hailed as an important step forward in Skunk Ape research.

The Skunk Ape Research Headquarters: The Skunk Ape Research Headquarters, located in Ochopee, Florida, is a popular destination for Skunk Ape enthusiasts and researchers. The headquarters features a museum and gift shop, as well as a campground and research center. The site has been the location of several reported Skunk Ape sightings over the years, and is considered by many to be a hub of Skunk Ape activity.

Overall, this chapter will explore the role of eyewitness testimony and physical evidence in Skunk Ape research, and will provide a detailed examination of some of the most compelling Skunk Ape sightings and encounters on record.

Throughout the years, there have been many reported sightings and encounters with the Skunk Ape throughout Florida and the southeastern United States. While some of these accounts have been dismissed as hoaxes or misidentifications of known animals, others remain unexplained to this day.

One of the most famous sightings of the Skunk Ape occurred in 1974, when a woman named Myakka Jane claimed to have seen the creature in the Myakka River State Park in Sarasota, Florida. According to Jane, she was driving along a deserted road in the park when she saw a large, hairy creature standing in the middle of the road. The creature was about seven feet tall, covered in reddish-brown hair, and emitted a foul odor that smelled like rotten eggs.

Jane's account of the encounter quickly spread throughout the local community, and soon, other residents began reporting their own sightings of the creature in the area. Despite numerous searches by local authorities and cryptozoologists, no concrete evidence was ever found to support the existence of the Skunk Ape in the area.

In 2000, a man named Dave Shealy claimed to have captured video footage of the Skunk Ape in the Everglades National Park. Shealy, who runs a wildlife sanctuary in the area, had been searching for the creature for over 20 years when he finally caught a glimpse of it on film. The footage shows a large, hairy creature walking through the swamp, but the quality of the video is poor, and it is difficult to make out any clear details of the creature.

Since then, there have been numerous other reported sightings of the Skunk Ape throughout the southeastern United States, with eyewitnesses describing encounters with a large, ape-like creature that emits a strong, foul odor. Some researchers believe that these sightings may be the result of misidentified known animals, such as bears or large apes that have escaped from captivity. Others, however, argue that the Skunk Ape may be a completely new species that has yet to be discovered and properly classified by science.

Despite the lack of concrete evidence to support the existence of the Skunk Ape, many people remain convinced that the creature is real, and sightings and encounters with the creature continue to be reported to this day. As we explore the evidence and stories surrounding the Skunk Ape in the following chapters, we'll delve deeper into the mysteries and controversies surrounding this elusive creature.

PHYSICAL EVIDENCE

In addition to the reported sightings and encounters with the Skunk Ape, there have also been several alleged tracks and other physical evidence found in areas where the creature is said to reside.

One such example is the Skunk Ape Research Center in Ochopee, Florida, which was established by Dave Shealy in 1997. The center features a collection of photographs, videos, and other items related to the Skunk Ape, as well as several casts of footprints that have been attributed to the creature. The footprints are said to be much larger than those of any known primate, measuring up to 17 inches in length and 8 inches in width.

Another purported piece of physical evidence is a photograph taken in 2000 by a woman named Linda J. Cunninham. The photo shows what appears to be a large, hairy creature standing in a swampy area, with its back turned to the camera. While the authenticity of the photograph has been widely debated, many Skunk Ape enthusiasts believe that it provides compelling evidence of the creature's existence.

Despite the various pieces of evidence that have been presented over the years, skeptics remain unconvinced that the Skunk Ape is a real animal. Many argue that the reported sightings and encounters with the creature are the result of hoaxes, misidentifications, or simply the imagination of those who claim to have seen it.

Regardless of whether the Skunk Ape is a real animal or a product of myth and legend, the creature continues to capture the imagination of people around the world. In the following chapters, we'll explore the various theories and controversies surrounding the Skunk Ape, as well as the ongoing efforts to uncover the truth behind this elusive creature.

In addition to the reported sightings and physical evidence, there have also been various attempts to capture or study the Skunk Ape. These efforts have included setting up camera traps in areas where the creature is said to reside, conducting aerial surveys to try and spot the creature from above, and even using trained dogs to track its scent.

One notable attempt to capture the Skunk Ape occurred in 1977, when a group of hunters from Alabama claimed to have captured one of the creatures alive in a trap. According to the hunters, they had set up a large cage baited with food and waited for the creature to enter. After several days, the trap was triggered, and the hunters found a large, hairy creature inside. However, before they could take any photographs or further examine the creature, it reportedly escaped from the cage and disappeared into the surrounding woods.

While many people remain skeptical of the hunters' story, others have pointed to the incident as possible evidence that the Skunk Ape is a real animal. However, without any physical evidence or documentation to support the hunters' claims, it is difficult to say for certain what really happened.

Despite the various attempts to capture or study the Skunk Ape, the creature remains elusive, and its existence continues to be shrouded in mystery. As we continue our exploration of the Skunk Ape in the following chapters, we'll examine the various theories and hypotheses that have been put forward in an attempt to explain this enigmatic creature, and we'll take a closer look at the ongoing efforts to uncover the truth behind its existence.

FAMOUS SKUNK APE SIGHTINGS

Over the years, there have been many reported sightings of the Skunk Ape in Florida and beyond. While some of these sightings may be hoaxes or misidentifications of other animals, there are several well-documented encounters that have captured the attention of researchers and enthusiasts alike.

The Myakka Skunk Ape Photo

One of the most famous and controversial Skunk Ape sightings occurred in 2000, when a woman named Rhonda Carlsen captured a photograph of a large, hairy creature in Myakka River State Park. The photo, which appears to show a bipedal creature with long arms and reddish-brown fur, quickly went viral and has been widely debated and analyzed ever since.

While some researchers believe that the photo is evidence of the Skunk Ape's existence, others argue that it is a hoax or a misidentification of a bear or other animal.

The Dave Shealy Encounters

Dave Shealy is a well-known Skunk Ape researcher and enthusiast who has had several encounters with the creature over the years. In one of his most famous encounters, which occurred in 1997, Shealy claims to have come face-to-face with a Skunk Ape while leading a group of tourists on a nature hike in the Everglades.

According to Shealy, the creature was approximately seven feet tall and covered in dark, matted fur. He also reported a strong, unpleasant odor, which is often associated with Skunk Ape sightings.

The Lettuce Lake Skunk Ape

In 2014, a group of teenagers reported seeing a large, ape-like creature near Lettuce Lake Park in Tampa, Florida. The teens were able to capture a brief video of the creature, which appears to show a large, bipedal animal walking through the woods.

While the video is not clear enough to definitively identify the creature as a Skunk Ape, it has been cited as evidence of the creature's existence by some researchers and enthusiasts.

The Skunk Ape Swamp Ape Game Camera Footage

In 2020, a game camera captured footage of a large, hairy creature walking through the woods near Big Cypress National Preserve in Florida. The footage, which was released by the Skunk Ape Research Headquarters, shows a large, bipedal creature with long arms and a distinctively ape-like gait.

While the footage is not clear enough to definitively identify the creature as a Skunk Ape, it has generated significant interest and speculation among researchers and enthusiasts. Some have even suggested that it may be the most compelling evidence of the creature's existence to date.

The Green Swamp Skunk Ape

In 2017, a group of researchers investigating reports of Skunk Ape sightings in the Green Swamp area of Florida claimed to have found evidence of the creature's existence. The team reportedly found large footprints, hair samples, and other physical evidence that they believe could be attributed to the Skunk Ape.

While some skeptics have dismissed the evidence as inconclusive or hoaxed, the researchers stand by their findings and continue to investigate the area for further evidence.

The Skunk Ape Research Headquarters

The Skunk Ape Research Headquarters, located in Ochopee, Florida, is a popular destination for Skunk

Ape enthusiasts and researchers. The headquarters, which is run by Dave Shealy and his family, features a museum of Skunk Ape artifacts and exhibits, as well as a gift shop and campground.

Many visitors to the Skunk Ape Research Headquarters claim to have had their own encounters with the creature, and the Shealy family continues to conduct research and investigate reported sightings in the surrounding area.

The Skunk Ape Research Consortium

The Skunk Ape Research Consortium is a group of researchers and enthusiasts who are dedicated to studying and documenting the Skunk Ape. The consortium was founded in 2009 and includes members from all over the world.

The group conducts field research, analyzes evidence, and hosts events and conferences related to the Skunk Ape. They also maintain a database of reported sightings and collaborate with other researchers and organizations to advance knowledge of the creature.

Overall, the Skunk Ape remains a mysterious and elusive creature, with many unanswered questions and debates surrounding its existence. However, the reported sightings and evidence continue to intrigue and captivate researchers and enthusiasts, keeping the legend of the Skunk Ape alive.

CHAPTER 4:
SCIENTIFIC
INVESTIGATIONS

Despite the many years of research and investigation into the Skunk Ape, there is still much to learn about this mysterious creature. As technology and scientific methods continue to advance, there may be new opportunities to study and understand the Skunk Ape in greater detail.

Some researchers and enthusiasts are currently using advanced surveillance equipment, such as motion-activated cameras and drones, to track and monitor the creature in its natural habitat. Others are studying DNA samples and physical evidence, in the hopes of uncovering new insights into the Skunk Ape's biology and origins.

Cryptozoologists are researchers who specialize in the study of animals that have not yet been officially recognized by science. The Skunk Ape is one of the many cryptids that fall into this category, along with creatures such as Bigfoot, the Loch Ness Monster, and the Chupacabra.

In recent years, there have been numerous reports of sightings and encounters with the Skunk Ape throughout the southeastern United States. Many of these reports come from hunters, hikers, and other outdoor enthusiasts who claim to have seen the creature while exploring the wilderness.

Despite the lack of concrete evidence to support the existence of the Skunk Ape, many people remain convinced that the creature is real. Some researchers believe that the Skunk Ape may be a surviving population of prehistoric apes that have somehow managed to avoid detection by humans for thousands of years.

Others speculate that the Skunk Ape may be a product of genetic experimentation or a mutated animal that has somehow adapted to life in the Florida swamps. Still, others believe that the Skunk Ape may be a supernatural entity, capable of appearing and disappearing at will, and possessing a variety of otherworldly powers.

One of the biggest challenges facing Skunk Ape research is the lack of physical evidence. While there have been reported sightings and encounters with the creature, there is little concrete evidence to support the existence of the Skunk Ape. Without physical evidence, it is difficult to conduct rigorous scientific research and gain a deeper understanding of the creature's biology and behavior.

Despite these challenges, there are several potential avenues for future Skunk Ape research. One promising area of study is DNA analysis. With advances in genetic sequencing technology, it may be possible to obtain DNA samples from hair, feces, or other biological materials attributed to the Skunk Ape. By analyzing this DNA, researchers could gain insight into the creature's genetic makeup and relationship to other primates.

Another potential area of study is the use of remote sensing technology. Drones, thermal imaging cameras, and other remote sensing technologies could be used to search for and track the Skunk Ape, potentially providing new insights into its behavior and habitat.

Finally, there is a growing interest in using citizen science and community-based research to study the Skunk Ape. By engaging with local communities and enlisting the help of volunteers, researchers could gather data and insights that would be difficult to obtain through traditional scientific methods.

The Skunk Ape has been the subject of much speculation and debate over the years, with a wide variety of theories and explanations being put forward to explain the creature's existence. In this chapter, we'll explore some of the most popular theories and hypotheses, as well as examine the evidence that supports or contradicts them.

Cryptozoology

One of the most popular explanations for the Skunk Ape is that it is a type of undiscovered primate, similar to the more well-known Bigfoot or Yeti. This theory is based on the many reported sightings and encounters with the creature, as well as the physical evidence that has been collected over the years.

Cryptozoologists, who study animals that are believed to exist but have not yet been scientifically proven, believe that the Skunk Ape could be a member of the great ape family, such as a new species of orangutan or a type of undiscovered gorilla. Proponents of this theory point to the creature's reported physical characteristics, such as its large size, hairy body, and ape-like features, as evidence that it is a real animal.

Hoaxes and Misidentifications

Another popular theory is that the Skunk Ape is simply the result of hoaxes or misidentifications. Skeptics argue that many of the reported sightings and encounters with the creature are either deliberate hoaxes or are the result of people misidentifying known animals, such as bears or feral hogs.

There have been several cases over the years where individuals have admitted to creating fake Skunk Ape sightings or tracks, either as a practical joke or to draw attention to a particular area. Additionally, some skeptics argue that the reported sightings of the creature could be attributed to the misidentification of known animals, particularly in low light or other difficult viewing conditions.

Supernatural or Paranormal Explanations

Some proponents of the Skunk Ape believe that the creature possesses supernatural or paranormal abilities, such as the ability to become invisible or to teleport. These theories are often based on reported sightings or encounters where the creature seemed to disappear or move in ways that defy explanation.

While there is no scientific evidence to support

these theories, they continue to be popular among some Skunk Ape enthusiasts. However, skeptics argue that these reported sightings and encounters could be the result of misinterpretations or misunderstandings of natural phenomena.

Environmental or Biological Explanations

Finally, some researchers have put forward environmental or biological explanations for the Skunk Ape. These theories suggest that the creature could be a product of environmental factors, such as pollution or habitat destruction, or could be the result of genetic abnormalities or other biological factors.

While these theories are less popular than others, they continue to be studied by some researchers in an attempt to uncover the truth behind the Skunk Ape. However, without more concrete evidence to support these theories, they remain largely speculative.

In the following chapters, we'll take a closer look at some of the evidence and arguments for and against these various theories, and we'll examine the ongoing efforts to study and understand the elusive Skunk Ape.

Government Conspiracy Theories

Some individuals and groups have put forward the theory that the Skunk Ape is being covered up or hidden by the government, either to protect national security or to prevent panic among the public. Proponents of this theory point to the many reported sightings of the creature, as well as the lack of official acknowledgement or investigation, as evidence that the government is actively concealing information about the Skunk Ape.

While there is no concrete evidence to support these theories, they continue to be popular among conspiracy theorists and Skunk Ape enthusiasts who believe that the truth about the creature is being deliberately hidden from the public.

Cultural Significance

The Skunk Ape has become a significant part of Florida's cultural identity, with many people viewing the creature as an important symbol of the state's natural heritage. The creature has been featured in numerous works of art, literature, and popular culture, and has even been adopted as a mascot by some Florida-based sports teams and businesses.

The cultural significance of the Skunk Ape has also led to a renewed interest in the creature among researchers and enthusiasts, who see it as an important part of Florida's history and folklore. This renewed interest has led to a number of new sightings and encounters being reported, as well as increased efforts to study and understand the elusive creature.

Overall, the Skunk Ape remains a mysterious and enigmatic creature, with no clear explanation for its existence. While there are a wide variety of theories and explanations, each with their own evidence and arguments, the truth about the Skunk Ape remains elusive. However, the ongoing efforts to study and understand the creature continue, and who knows what new discoveries and insights may be uncovered in the future.

CHAPTER 5: SKUNK APE IN POP CULTURE AND MEDIA

Overall, this chapter will provide an overview of the various ways in which the Skunk Ape has been represented and interpreted in popular culture and media. By examining these representations, we can gain a deeper understanding of the role that the Skunk Ape plays in our collective imagination and cultural landscape.

The Skunk Ape has become a popular subject in pop culture and media, appearing in everything from movies and TV shows to video games and music. In this chapter, we will explore the ways in which the Skunk Ape has been represented and interpreted in various forms of media.

The Skunk Ape has made appearances in various forms of popular culture, including books, television shows, and films. Some examples include the children's book "The Skunk Ape and the Sasquatch" by Glen Huser, the TV series "Finding Bigfoot," and the horror film "Skunk Ape Lives!"

While these depictions of the Skunk Ape are often fictional, they help to keep the legend of the creature alive and raise awareness about the ongoing research and investigation into its existence.

One of the earliest examples of the Skunk Ape

appearing in popular culture is the 1977 movie "Creature from Black Lake," which tells the story of two college students searching for the Skunk Ape in Louisiana. Since then, the Skunk Ape has appeared in a variety of movies and TV shows, including "Lost Tapes," "Monsters and Mysteries in America," and "Finding Bigfoot."

The Skunk Ape has also appeared in literature, with authors such as Tim Dorsey and Carl Hiaasen including references to the creature in their books. In addition, the Skunk Ape has been the subject of numerous songs and albums, with bands such as the Red Elvises and the Dark Water Rebellion referencing the creature in their music.

Another way in which the Skunk Ape has been represented in popular culture is through merchandise and branding. T-shirts, hats, and other items featuring the Skunk Ape have become popular among enthusiasts, and the creature has even been used as a mascot for various businesses and events.

Skunk Ape Tourism

The legend of the Skunk Ape has also become a significant part of Florida's tourism industry. Many visitors to the state are drawn to areas where the creature has been reported, in the hopes of catching a glimpse or experiencing a sighting themselves. This has led to the development of Skunk Ape-themed attractions, tours, and merchandise, which cater to both tourists and locals alike.

Some of the most popular Skunk Ape attractions in Florida include the Skunk Ape Research Headquarters in Ochopee, which features a museum, gift shop, and educational programs, as well as the annual Skunk Ape Festival in Collier County, which celebrates the legend with live music, food, and other entertainment.

While some critics argue that the commercialization of the Skunk Ape legend detracts from its authenticity and significance, others see it as a way to promote interest in the creature and support local businesses and communities.

While the Skunk Ape has been the subject of numerous works of fiction and media, it is important to remember that these representations may not accurately reflect the reality of the creature (if it indeed exists). As such, it is important to approach representations of the Skunk Ape in media with a critical eye, and to recognize that these interpretations are often influenced by cultural and historical contexts.

CHAPTER 6:
THE FUTURE
OF SKUNK APE
RESEARCH

The Skunk Ape legend has captivated the imaginations of people for generations, but what does the future hold for Skunk Ape research? In this chapter, we will explore some of the challenges and opportunities facing Skunk Ape researchers and enthusiasts, and discuss potential avenues for future research.

Technological Advancements

Advances in technology may play a key role in Skunk Ape research in the future. For example, drones equipped with high-resolution cameras may be able to survey large areas of wilderness and capture images of any elusive creatures. DNA analysis techniques may also become more advanced, allowing researchers to examine hair and tissue samples for evidence of the creature's existence.

Increased Awareness and Support

As more people become aware of the Skunk Ape and the ongoing research into its existence, there may be increased support for conservation efforts and funding for further research. Public interest in the creature may also lead to an increase in reported sightings and evidence, further fueling the investigation.

Continued Collaboration and Cooperation

Skunk Ape research is a collaborative effort, with researchers, enthusiasts, and conservation organizations working together to uncover the truth about the creature. Continued cooperation and collaboration among these groups will be important for the future of Skunk Ape research, as they work together to share information and resources.

The Possibility of Discovery

Perhaps the most exciting prospect for the future of Skunk Ape research is the possibility of a genuine discovery. If a creature matching the description of the Skunk Ape is captured or documented, it could provide conclusive evidence of its existence and pave the way for further study.

Increased Public Interest

As the Skunk Ape gains more media attention and becomes a popular topic in the paranormal and cryptozoology communities, there is likely to be an increase in public interest as well. This may lead to more people taking an active interest in Skunk Ape research, as well as increased support for conservation efforts in the areas where the creature is believed to live.

Encroaching Human Development

One challenge for Skunk Ape research in the future

may be the impact of human development on the creature's habitat. As urbanization and other forms of human encroachment continue to spread into natural areas, the Skunk Ape's habitat may be reduced or fragmented. This could make it more difficult for researchers to find and study the creature, as well as putting its survival at risk.

Cultural Significance

The Skunk Ape is an important part of the folklore and cultural heritage of Florida and other areas where it is believed to exist. As such, Skunk Ape research has implications beyond the purely scientific or academic, and may have cultural, historical, and social significance as well. By uncovering the truth behind the legend, Skunk Ape research may help to preserve and celebrate these cultural traditions for future generations.

Ethical Considerations

Finally, as with any research involving potentially unknown or undiscovered species, there are ethical considerations to be taken into account. Researchers must balance the potential benefits of Skunk Ape research with the need to protect and preserve the creature and its habitat. This may involve working with local communities and conservation organizations to develop sustainable research practices that prioritize the welfare of the Skunk Ape and its environment.

International Collaborations

The search for the Skunk Ape is not limited to Florida or the United States. Cryptozoologists and researchers from around the world have shown an interest in this elusive creature, and international collaborations may play a crucial role in Skunk Ape research in the future. These collaborations could bring together experts in a wide range of fields, including genetics, ecology, and wildlife management, to share knowledge and resources and develop more effective research strategies.

Funding Challenges

Skunk Ape research is a relatively underfunded field, with many researchers and enthusiasts working on a voluntary basis. In the future, there may be a need for increased funding to support more extensive and rigorous research into the creature's existence. This could come from government agencies, private foundations, or even crowdfunding campaigns. Funding could be used to support research projects, field studies, and conservation efforts, as well as to develop new technologies and methods for studying the Skunk Ape.

Conservation Efforts

As the Skunk Ape remains a mysterious and elusive creature, little is known about its population size, habitat, and conservation status. However, efforts are underway to protect the habitats in which it is believed to reside and to promote conservation of the natural environment.

Conservation organizations and researchers are working to document the flora and fauna of the Florida wilderness, including the Skunk Ape, in order to better understand their ecological significance and conservation needs. These efforts are important not only for the protection of the Skunk Ape, but for the overall health and wellbeing of the natural world.

Regardless of the truth behind the Skunk Ape legend, it continues to captivate the imaginations of people around the world. Whether it is a creature of myth or a real animal that has yet to be properly identified, the Skunk Ape remains a fascinating and enduring mystery of the natural world. In the following chapters, we'll explore the evidence and stories surrounding this elusive creature in more detail, in an attempt to uncover the truth behind the legend.

HOAXES AND MISIDENTIFICATIONS

While there have been many reported sightings of the Skunk Ape over the years, not all of them are genuine. Some sightings may be hoaxes, perpetrated by individuals looking for attention or attempting to create a stir. Others may be misidentifications of known animals or objects.

For example, some sightings of the Skunk Ape may actually be of feral hogs or bears, which can be mistaken for the creature due to their size and appearance. Additionally, some reports of Skunk Ape sightings may be attributed to misidentification of people wearing fur costumes or other disguises.

It is important for researchers and enthusiasts to carefully consider and evaluate the evidence before accepting a sighting as genuine. This helps to maintain the credibility of the field and ensure that genuine sightings are given the attention they deserve.

SKEPTICS AND DEBUNKERS

As with any paranormal or cryptozoological phenomenon, there are those who remain skeptical of the Skunk Ape's existence. Skeptics and debunkers argue that the evidence put forward by researchers and enthusiasts is inconclusive or easily explained by other means.

Some skeptics argue that the sightings of the Skunk Ape are the result of misidentification, hoaxes, or the natural inclination of the human brain to see patterns and connections where there are none. Others argue that the Skunk Ape is simply a modern variation on ancient mythological creatures such as the Wild Man or Bigfoot.

Despite the skepticism, however, the legend of the Skunk Ape continues to endure, with sightings and evidence continuing to be reported by researchers and enthusiasts around the world.

CONCLUSION:

The legend of the Skunk Ape continues to captivate the imagination of people around the world, with reports of sightings and evidence continuing to emerge. While the existence of the creature remains a mystery, ongoing research and investigation provide hope for a future discovery. Whether the Skunk Ape is a supernatural being or a real, undiscovered species, the search for the truth behind the legend is sure to continue for years to come.

Disclaimer:

The information contained in this book is intended to be educational and informative. While every effort has been made to ensure that the content is accurate and up-to-date, the author and publisher make no guarantees regarding the completeness, accuracy, or suitability of the information presented.

The content in this book is based on a combination of research, personal experience, and anecdotal evidence, and should not be construed as medical, legal, or professional advice. The author and publisher are not liable for any damages or losses that may arise from the use or reliance on the information presented in this book.

Additionally, some of the illustrations in this book were generated using artificial intelligence (AI) and are intended to be artistic representations of the Skunk Ape. While we have made every effort to ensure that these illustrations are respectful and accurate representations of the Skunk Ape, they are not intended to be scientifically accurate depictions of this cryptid. The opinions and interpretations of the Skunk Ape presented in this book are based on folklore and personal accounts, and may not reflect the viewpoints of all readers.

This disclaimer is intended to provide clarity and transparency regarding the content of the book and the use of AI-generated illustrations, and to protect both the author and publisher from any legal liability or damages that may arise from the use of the information presented in this book.